COLLECTIONS

A Harcourt Reading / Language Arts Program

DECODABLE BOOK
BOOK 1-2

Harcourt

Orlando   Boston   Dallas   Chicago   San Diego

Visit *The Learning Site!*

www.hbschool.com

Contents

Dot and Pom-Pom

by Suzanne Weyn
illustrated by Wallace Keller

Dot is sick.

Pom-Pom is not!

2

Pom-Pom hops up.
"Sit, Pom-Pom! I
need a nap."

Pom-Pom sits on
Dot! Dot can't nap.

4

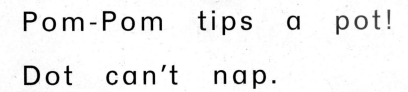

Pom-Pom tips a pot!

Dot can't nap.

Pom-Pom has Dot's sock! Dot can't nap.

POM

7

At last, Dot can nap.

8

Where Is Nan?

by Amy E. Weingartner

illustrated by
Joung
Un Kim

Where is Nan? Nan
is not on this mat.

Thad calls Nan. Nan!
Thad and Mom look
on the path.

Mom calls Nan. Nan!
Look at that! That is
not Nan.

12

Hop! Hop! Hop!
This is not Nan.

Thad and Mom call
Nan. Nan! Nan!

Is that Nan?

Nan is here.

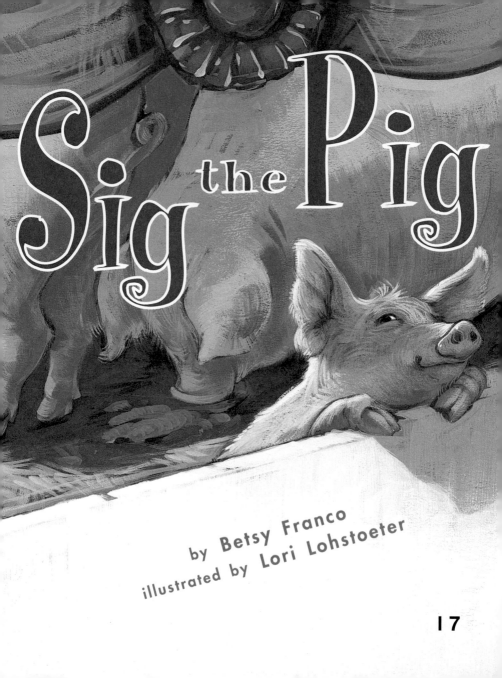

Sig the Pig

the

by **Betsy** Franco
illustrated by **Lori** Lohstoeter

Sig is a small pig.

Sig is a hot pig.

Sig digs and digs.

Now Sig is not hot.

Sig has a snack.

Sig is not thin.

23

Look at that—and
Sig is still growing!

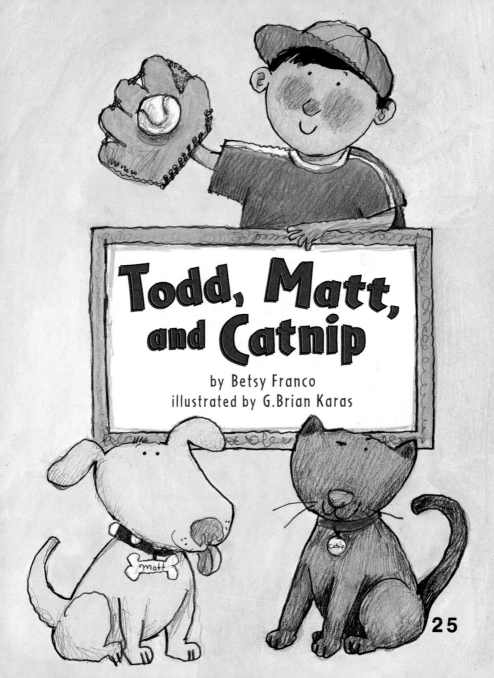

Todd, Matt, and Catnip

by Betsy Franco

illustrated by G. Brian Karas

Todd packed mitts, caps, and snacks.

"Come, on, Matt!" called Todd.

"Catnip, you can't come."

Todd and Matt passed a hill.

Catnip passed the hill, too.

"Todd has mitts!" called Ann.

"Matt has caps!" called Scott.

Catnip had the snacks!

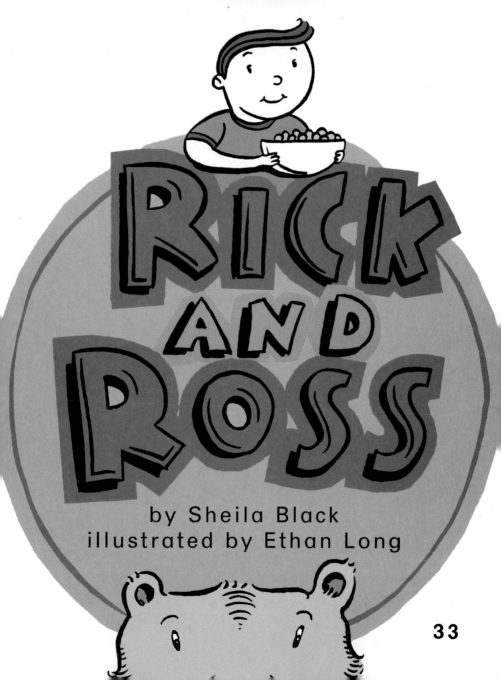

RICK AND ROSS

by Sheila Black
illustrated by Ethan Long

Rick has a pal.
Is it a cat? Is
it a dog?

Rick's pal is small.

Rick calls him Ross.

Ross is on the rock.

"Ross," Rick calls,
and Ross hops on
his hand.

Ross can do tricks.

Now Ross is sad.

Where's Rick?

Here's Rick! Rick
and Ross are pals!

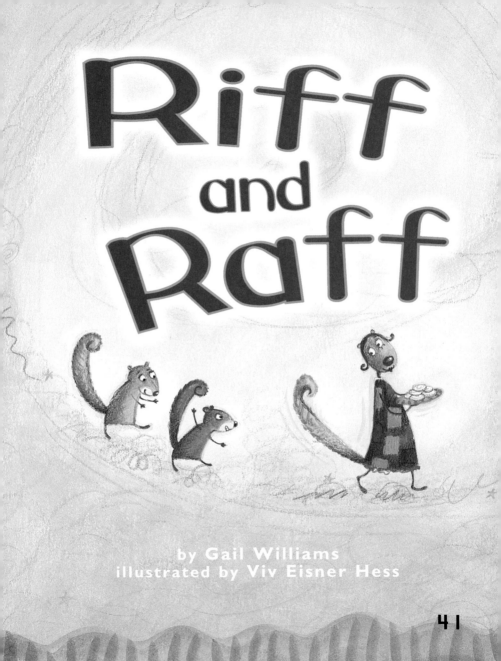

Riff
and
Raff

by Gail Williams
illustrated by Viv Eisner Hess

Sniff, sniff.

Sniff, sniff. Riff and
Raff sniff a snack.

Riff is fast! So is Raff.

Riff falls on the fan.

Raff falls on the pan.

Riff falls off the fan.

Raff falls off the pan.

"Where is Riff?" thinks
Raff. "Where is Raff?"
thinks Riff.

46

"Where is the snack?"
thinks Mom.

"Riff! Raff!" calls Mom.

"It is NOT snack time!"

Hit It, Rabbit!

by Barbara Sobel
illustrated by Wong Herbert Yee

Rabbit is at bat.

Pig grabs the ball.

"I can hit it," thinks
Rabbit. "I can hit
that ball."

"Rabbit can't hit it,"
thinks Pig. "Rabbit
can't hit this ball."

Pig tossed the ball.

"I missed it," sobs
Rabbit. Pig has a
big grin.

Pig tossed a
fast ball. BAM!

"Rabbit blasted it,"
sobs Pig. Now Rabbit
has the big grin!

Morning Song

by Mary Hogan ✹ illustrated by Nancy Davis

In the morning, Doris
sings and claps.

In his fort, Todd
sings and taps.

Sing! Sing a morning song!

Gram rocks back
and forth.

Nan spins in the north.

Sing! Sing a morning song!

In   the   tall   corn,
Norm   flips   and   flops.

In a storm,
Ann skips and hops.

Sing! Sing a morning song!

Who is singing?

Is it you?

Sing! Sing a morning song, too!

King Wick Plays Ball

by J.C. Cunningham

illustrated by Bill Mayer

65

King Wick puts on his wig.

"Wags!" King Wick
calls. "Come with me."

King Wick will play
ball. Wags will sit.

King Wick kicks. Smack!
Good kick, King Wick!

Smack!
King Wick kicks,
twists, and spins. King
Wick will hit the grass.

The ball
will hit the wall.

Where is that ball?

Is it lost?

Wags has it! Wags wins!

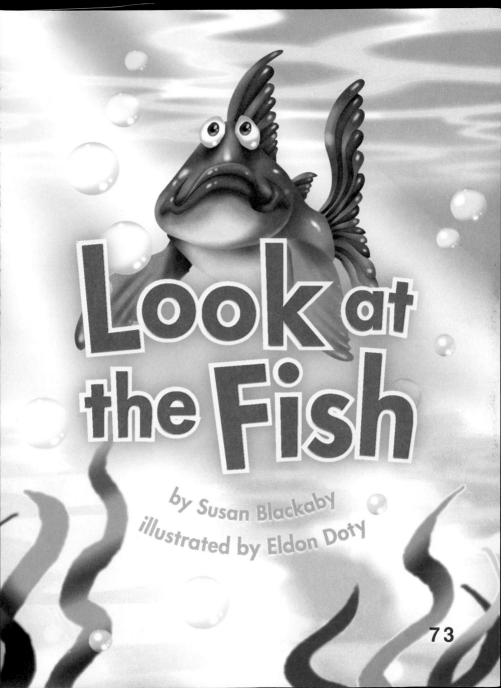

Look at the Fish

by Susan Blackaby
illustrated by Eldon Doty

Look at all the fish!
Swim, fish, swim!

That fish swims fast.
It is long, too.

This fish has spots.

It is tan and pink.

That small fish hid.

It swam in that hole.

Look at that thin fish. It is swimming on that path.

Did you see that fish?

It is called a catfish.

Look at all the fish—
long fish, fish with
spots, small fish, and
thin fish!

At the Pond

by **Amy E. Weingartner**

illustrated by **Hanako Wakiyama**

Ben and his dad set
up camp. Ben helps
Dad with the tent.

Then Ben and Dad
dash to the pond.
It has lots of tall
plants with long stems.

Frogs hop and swim in the pond. Fish swim in the pond as well.

"All fish have fins,"
Dad tells Ben. "Fins
help them swim."

"Ben," calls Dad,
"look at all the
fish eggs."

Ben bends down.
"Watch your step,"
Dad tells Ben.

Splash! Plop! Ben gets
wet! "I am a fish with
legs!" Ben tells Dad.

MAX AND ROXANN

by Suzanne Weyn

illustrated by Michael Letzig

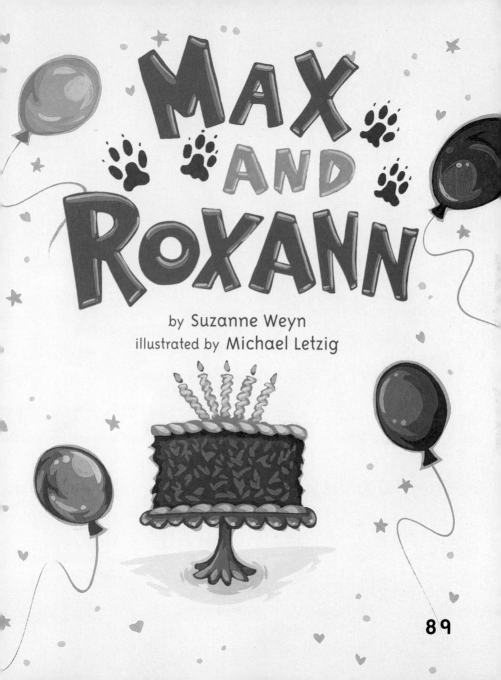

Max got a big, red
fox. Max called his
fox Roxann.

Max got a box for
Roxann's bed.

Max put some things
in the box.

"This is your bed,
Roxann. This is the
best bed for a fox."

Max patted his big, red fox. "Let's nap, Roxann."

Max looked at Roxann.

Roxann looked at Max.

Max can rest in his big
bed. Roxann can rest in
the big bed, too.